Matter and Its

by Timothy Sandow

How can we describe matter?

A World of Matter

All of the things you see around you are made of matter. **Matter** is anything that takes up space and has mass. You can sense the mass of an object by how heavy it feels. You can see that air takes up space when you blow up a balloon.

A **property** is something about matter that you can see, hear, touch, or smell. A ball looks round. It feels smooth or bumpy. It can be hard or soft. It makes a sound when you bounce it. You can smell a flower to learn about its properties.

States of Matter

Nearly all matter is a solid, a liquid, or a gas. Each kind of matter is made of very tiny particles. The particles are so small that we cannot see them. The particles are always moving. In some kinds of matter, they move a little. In other kinds of matter, they move a lot.

Solids

A bowling ball is a solid. Like other solids, it keeps its shape. It stays round. In a solid, all the tiny particles are firmly held together. They jiggle very fast, but they stay in place.

Solid particles that jiggle in place

Liquid particles that slide past each other

Liquids

Orange juice is a liquid. It takes the shape of the glass it is in. It will take a new shape if poured into a different glass. The particles of liquids are loosely held together. The particles can flow past one another. What if you poured the juice into a new container? It will still take up the same amount of space.

Gases

Gases do not have a shape. Air is a gas. Tiny gas particles are not connected to each other. They bounce off each other as they move freely in space. Unlike solids and liquids, the amount of space that air takes up can change.

When air is pumped into a ball, it expands. It pushes against the inside of the ball. This pushing is called **pressure.** The air particles get more tightly pressed together as you pump more air in.

Gas particles that bounce off each other

Parts of Matter

What happens if you break a chunk of gold into smaller pieces? Each particle of gold is still the matter gold. Gold is an element. An **element** is matter made of a single type of particle too small to see.

Most matter is made out of many types of particles. The smallest particle of an element that has all the properties of that element is an **atom.** Gold is made up only of atoms of gold. Clay is an example of matter made up of different kinds of atoms. Atoms act together to give matter its properties.

Clay is made of many different kinds of atoms.

Periodic Table of Elements

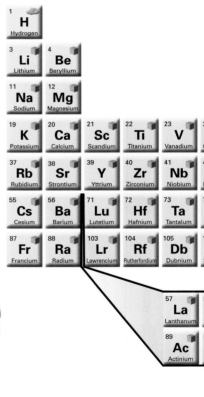

Scientists have done experiments to find out how many different elements there are in matter. Their experiments show that there are more than one hundred different elements. Scientists list all these elements in a table. It is called the **periodic table** of elements. The elements are placed on the table near other elements with the same properties.

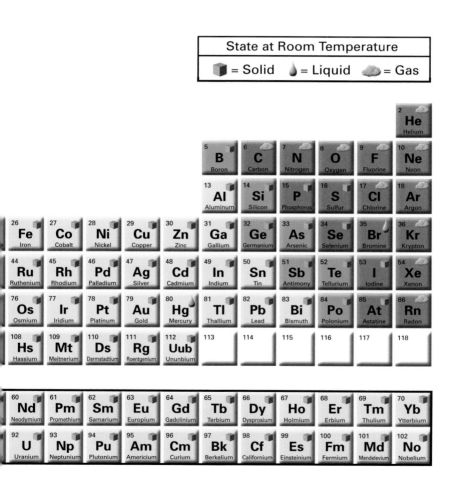

How are properties of matter measured?

Tools for Measuring Mass

One property of matter that you can measure is mass. **Mass** is the amount of matter an object has. A balance measures mass. The metric units for measuring mass are grams (g) and kilograms (kg). One kilogram has 1,000 grams.

An object's mass is the same no matter where it is. But the weight of an object can be different in different places. Things have different weights on Earth than they do on the Moon. A scale is used to measure weight.

A balance measures mass. The whole toy has the same mass as its parts.

Tools for Measuring Volume

Another property of matter you can measure is volume. The **volume** of an object is the amount of space that the object takes up. You use a measuring cup or graduated cylinder to measure the volume of liquids.

The metric unit for measuring the volume of a liquid is the liter (L). We can also measure small amounts of liquid in milliliters (mL). One liter has 1,000 milliliters.

The volume of the milk in this jug is about 2L.

The volume of orange juice in this bottle is about 1L.

Solids have volume, just as liquids do. To measure the volume of a solid, fill a measuring cup half full of water. Record the measurement. Now, place a rock into the water. The water rises because the rock has volume. It takes up space. Look at the water level now. Record the new measurement. Subtract the first measurement from the second. The difference in the water levels is the volume of the rock.

The volume of the water in this measuring cup is 500 mL.

Measuring Density

Density is a measure of the amount of matter in a certain amount of space. A bowling ball and a rubberball have about the same volume. But the bowling ball has more mass and greater density.

You can study the density of matter by watching how an object floats. How well an object floats in a liquid or a gas is called **buoyancy.** Stones have little buoyancy in water. They sink because they have a higher density than water. A helium balloon has lots of buoyancy in air. It rises because helium has a lower density than air.

This rubber ball is the same size as the bowling ball.

Tools for Measuring Other Properties

Size is another property that can be measured. The distance from one end of something to the other is its length. The basic unit for measuring length is the meter (m). We use millimeters (mm) and centimeters (cm) to measure small things. One meter is 100 cm or 1,000 mm. We use kilometers (km) to measure long distances. One kilometer is 1,000 meters.

A cubic unit is a cube used to measure volume of a solid. A cube that is 1 centimeter on all sides has the volume of 1 cubic centimeter. To find the volume of a box, put cubes of the same size into the box, and fill it. The volume of the box is a measurement of how many cubic units it takes to fill the box.

Some objects are too small to see easily. Use a magnifying glass to make things look larger. Then you can see their properties better.

Glossary

atom
the smallest particle of a substance that has the properties of that substance

buoyancy
how well an object floats in a liquid or rises in air or a gas

density
how much matter is in a certain amount of space

element
a substance made up of a single type of particle

mass
the amount of matter any object contains

matter
anything that takes up space and has weight

periodic table
a table that arranges the elements of matter according to their properties

pressure
how hard something presses on something else

property
something about an object that can be observed

volume
the amount of space an object takes up